J 625.1
DIX
   Dixon, Malcolm
      On the railway

DATE DUE			
OC 20 '84	AUG 0 1 1994		
DE 29 '84			
NO 30 '85			
JUN 4 1988			
NOV 26 1988			
APR 6 1991			
DEC 14 1991			
MAR 7 1992			
MAR 2 0 1993			

(20)

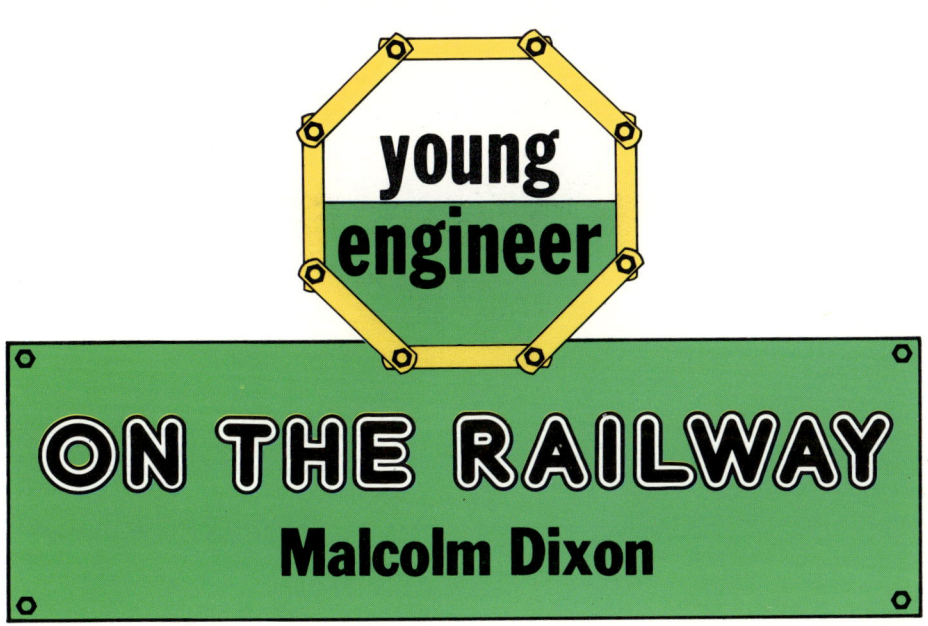

The Bookwright Press
New York · 1984

Young Engineer Series

- At Sea
- In the Home
- In the Air
- On the Road
- On the Waterway
- In the Factory
- On the Railroad
- In Communication

Adult supervision is suggested for some of the experiments in the Young Engineer series.

First published in the United States in 1984 by
The Bookwright Press, 387 Park Avenue South, New York, NY 10016

© Copyright 1983 by
Wayland (Publishers) Limited
All rights reserved
First published in 1983 by
Wayland (Publishers) Limited
49 Lansdowne Place, Hove
East Sussex BN3 1HF, England
ISBN 531-04795-4
Library of Congress Catalog Card Number 83-72791

Designed by Alan Gatland
Illustrated by Gerald Wood
Filmset by Latimer Trend & Company Ltd, Plymouth
Printed in Italy by G. Canale & C.S.p.A.

Contents

Chapter 1   Looking at railroads
Passenger and freight trains   4
Problems to solve   5

Chapter 2   Railroad tracks
Rails   6
Expansion   7
Different gauges   8
Keeping to the rails   9
Points   10

Chapter 3   Overcoming problems
Steep slopes   11
Embankments and cuttings   12
Bridges   13
Make a model bridge   14
Tunnels   15

Chapter 4   Power for the railroads
Steam power   16
Electric power   18
Diesel power   20

Chapter 5   Special trains
High-speed trains   21
Make a hovertrain   22
Mag-lev trains   23
Cable railways   24
Monorail trains   26
Underground trains   27

Chapter 6   Safety on the railroads
Railroads and cold weather   28
Simple signals   29
Make an electric signal   30
Automatic control   32

Chapter 1 Looking at railroads

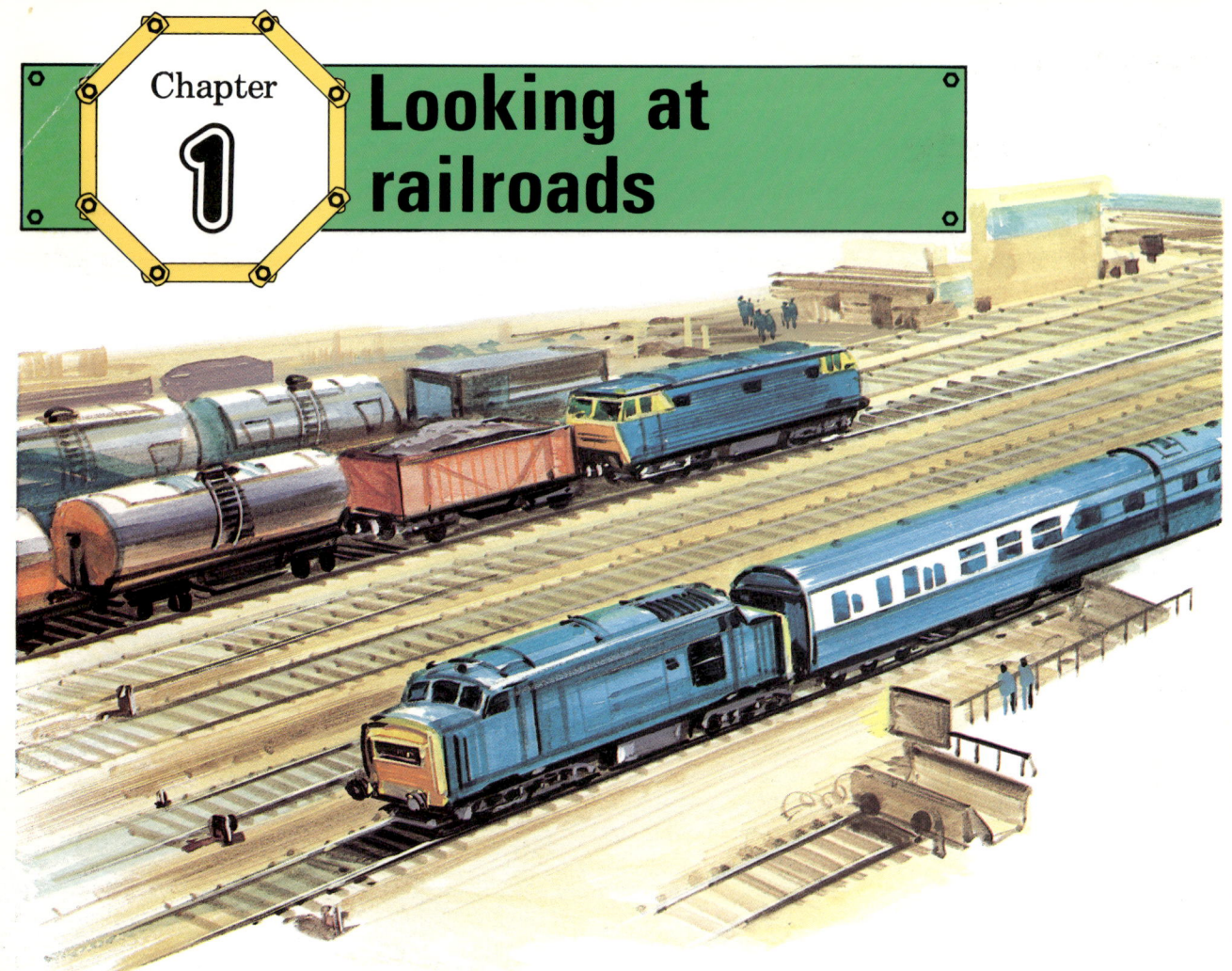

Passenger and freight trains

The building of the first railroads changed the lives of many people. These railroads allowed people to travel long distances safely and faster than by horse-drawn carriages. Goods, too, could now be carried on freight trains from factories and docks.

Today, railroads are still an important part of our lives. People use trains to travel to work and for pleasure. Freight trains carry many of the goods that need to be moved around the world.

Visit the railroad station nearest to your home. Look for passenger trains. Where are these trains coming from and going to?
How long do their journeys take?
How many times do the trains stop on each journey?
Can you see any freight trains?

Problems to solve

When building railroads, engineers have to solve many problems. Early engineers hired gangs of laborers who worked long hours to cut paths for the railroad tracks. They used simple tools, such as shovels, picks and wheelbarrows. Many men died building the railroads.

Engineers have built railroads covering vast distances. Sometimes the routes of these railroads have never been explored before. Often the engineers have to construct their routes through forests, tunnel through mountains and build bridges across rivers. Even though they use modern machinery, they still face many difficulties.

When you next travel on a train, think of the difficulties the engineers may have had building the railroad. How many tunnels do you travel through? How many bridges do you travel over? Do you pass through any deep gorges?

Chapter 2: Railroad tracks

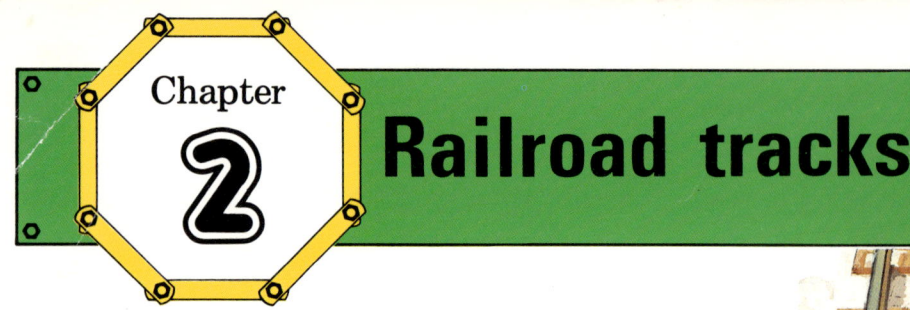

Rails

Modern trains run along steel rails. These rails are fastened to "sleepers" made from wood or concrete. When wood is used, it needs to be specially treated to prevent it from rotting.

Before laying the sleepers and steel rails, the engineers must prepare the land. The sleepers are laid on a foundation of broken stones, called ballast. Rainwater can drain through the stones, but they give the support needed for the massive weight of the trains on the rails.

Find a **safe** position to look at some railroad tracks. **Never go near the tracks.** Are the sleepers made of concrete or wood? How are the rails fastened to the sleepers? Notice how the sleepers are laid at right-angles to the rails.

 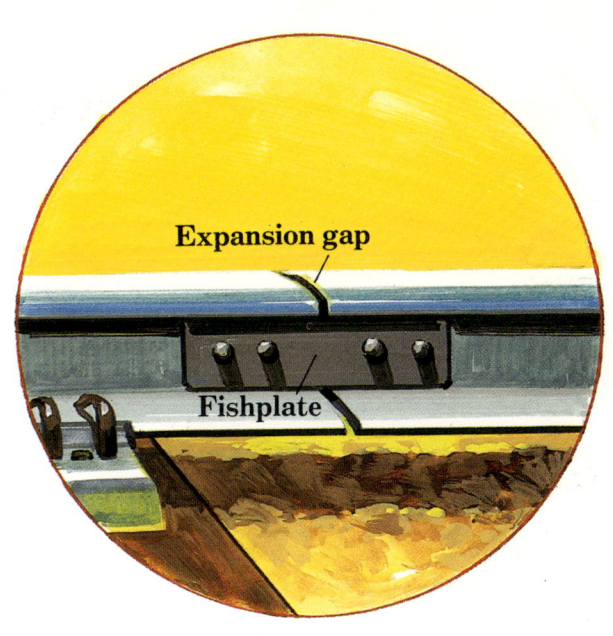

Expansion

Occasionally people have difficulty removing a metal screw lid from a jar. One way of getting the lid off is to hold it under some hot running water. The heat makes the lid slightly larger and it can be easily turned. We say that the metal lid has expanded. Try doing this if you find it difficult to unscrew a metal lid.

In hot weather, the rails on railroad tracks may also expand. This can make trains come off the rails and result in serious accidents. One way of preventing this is to leave small gaps where two rails join. When you travel in a train you can often hear the clatter as the wheels pass over these gaps. The two rails are held together by a pair of metal "fishplates." One is fixed on each side of the rail.

Modern steel rails can be welded together to form very long lengths. Provided that these rails are firmly fastened to heavy sleepers, there is no need for expansion gaps. Engineers have found that expansion of the metal does not move the rail. Without the regular gaps in the rails, train journeys are much quieter.

Next time you travel on a train, listen to the sound of the wheels passing along the rails. Can you hear the regular clatter of gaps in the rails or are you traveling on the modern longer rails?

Different gauges

The distance between the two railroad rails is called the gauge. In Britain, some early engineers built railroads with a gauge of 4ft 8½ins (about 1.23 meters). Other engineers used a broader gauge of 7ft (about 2.14 meters). They thought that this would let them run larger trains at higher speeds. The British Parliament eventually decided to use only a standard gauge of 4ft 8½ins throughout the country. This standard gauge is used in Europe and in the USA, but many countries still use a broader gauge.

Look for a miniature railroad in a fairground or amusement park. Does it have a narrow-gauge railroad track?

Keeping to the rails

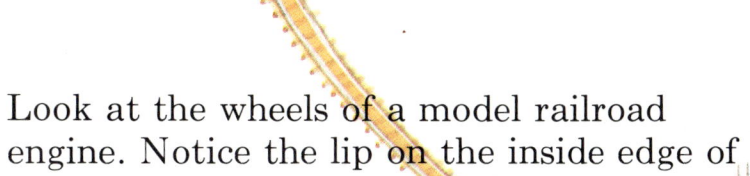

Look at the wheels of a model railroad engine. Notice the lip on the inside edge of each wheel. This lip is called a flange.

Place your engine on a model railroad track. Push the engine from the side with your finger. The flanges help to hold the engine on the track.

Look at the flanges on the steel wheels of full-sized trains. These flanges help trains to stay on the rails even when traveling around curves.

Engineers sometimes slightly lift the outer rails on curves. This gives the railroad track a tilt and helps to prevent train wheels from leaving the tracks.

Place some pieces of cardboard under the outer rails of one bend of a model railroad. Watch the train traveling around the track. Does the train ever come off the rails on the tilted bend? Try tilting the inner rail on a curve. What happens then?

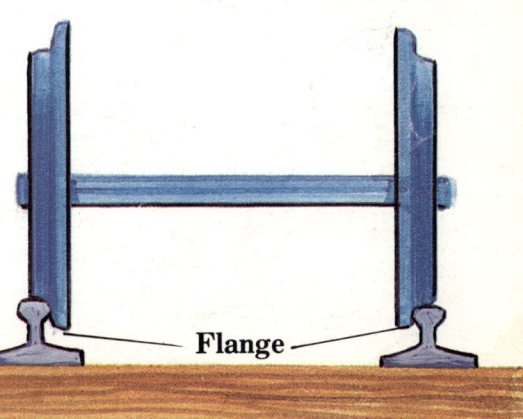

Cardboard under outer rail

Flange

Points

The place where two railroad tracks join is called a junction. So that a train can be directed onto either of the two tracks, railroad engineers build movable rails into the junction. These are called points.

Look at the points on a model railroad. Can you see the movable rails? Run a model locomotive across the points in the direction shown in the diagram below. Watch how the wheels follow the movable rails. What happens if you reverse the locomotive back over the points with the movable rails in the wrong position?

The points on your model railroad are probably worked by hand. Points on real railroads used to be operated by levers, but now they are mostly electronically operated.

Movable rails

Chapter 3
Overcoming problems

Steep slopes

Can a model train travel up a sloping track? Experiment to find out. Start with a slight slope. Support the track with pieces of cardboard. Try the experiment with just the engine and no freight cars or coaches. Use more cardboard pieces to gradually increase the slope. Watch the wheels. Can your model engine climb steep slopes? Now add some cars. Can the train climb such a steep slope?

The steel wheels of trains cannot grip the smooth steel rails of sloping tracks. The wheels slip, especially in wet weather. Engineers have tried to solve this problem by putting sand on to the rails. This helps the wheels to grip.

When very steep slopes have to be climbed in mountain areas, special toothed rails are sometimes used. One of these rails is fitted in the middle of the track. The trains are fitted with toothed gear wheels. These gear wheels fit into the toothed track and allow the train to climb the steep slopes safely.

When building railroads, engineers try to avoid the problems caused by sloping tracks. They do this by keeping the track as level as possible. This means that they have to build embankments, cuttings, tunnels and bridges.

Embankments and cuttings

Cutting

When there is a fall in the land level, the engineer may construct an embankment. This is a high bank of earth with a flat top. The track is laid along this level section. Are there any embankments near your home? How high are they? Do they have sloping sides?

Often the route of a railroad needs to cross hills. The engineer will dig through these hills to form cuttings to keep the line level. Today, explosives and excavating machines are used for this task. But in the past, gangs of laborers used picks and shovels to dig their way through the earth.

Embankment

Bridges

Bridges have to be built so that railroad lines can cross waterways, roads, gorges and other railroad lines. In some areas, massive wooden bridges have been built. Engineers have used timber for these bridges because many trees were growing near to the site of the bridge. These bridges are strong enough to carry heavy trains. But a big disadvantage is that the wood can easily catch fire.

This famous bridge below was built nearly one hundred years ago. It carries two railroad tracks over a very wide stretch of the River Forth in Scotland. It was built using, mainly, steel tubing.

This type of bridge is known as the "cantilever" design. Look for more railroad bridges. Make sketches of some of them. How many different types can you find?

13

Make a model bridge

Make a simple concrete bridge to use with a model railroad. Measure out a yogurt potful of cement, two pots of sand and three pots of small stones. Add half a pot of water and mix the materials together, using a piece of wood. Fill two small boxes with this mixture. Pat the top of each concrete mixture. This will push out any air bubbles. Leave both concrete mixtures to harden. Remove the hardened concrete pieces from both boxes.

Make a mold, using some pieces of wood. Mix more concrete and put it inside the wooden mold. Leave it to harden. Carefully remove the wooden supports. **Wash your hands with soap and water after mixing concrete.**

Place this concrete beam on the small concrete blocks. Arrange the track of a model railroad so that it travels over your concrete bridge. Use some cardboard or papier mâché to make embankments for the track. Make a road so that model cars can pass underneath the bridge.

Wooden moulds

Tunnels

Sometimes it is impossible to cut a path through a mountain or bridge a river. The engineer has to tunnel through the mountain and tunnel under the river.

The first railroad tunnels were dug by men working by candle-light. Horses helped to remove the debris. The invention of power drills helped the engineers to speed up the cutting of tunnels. But the men still worked in terrible conditions. Once the tunnels were built, some people were afraid to travel through them. They believed the tunnels would collapse and preferred to travel by another route.

Railroad tunnels have even been built through the highest mountains. They make it safer and quicker for people to travel in these areas.

Have you traveled through a railroad tunnel? Did it take you through some hills, a mountain or under a river?

Chapter 4: Power for the railroads

Steam power

The first steam locomotives were used to haul coal and other minerals from mines. In 1829, the British engineer George Stephenson and his son Robert built a locomotive, called the *Rocket*. This engine won a competition to find the best locomotive for the newly built Liverpool to Manchester railroad. For the next century, steam power was used to haul trains. In every steam locomotive, water is heated in a boiler. Steam from the boiler moves pistons in cylinders. This movement, by means of connecting rods, is used to turn the driving wheels of the engine. Most locomotives use coal for their fuel. The coal is burned in a firebox.

A steam locomotive needs to carry coal to burn in the firebox and water for the boiler. These are often carried in a wagon called a tender. This tender is pulled behind the locomotive. A railroadman, called a fireman, makes sure that the firebox is fed with coal.

The world speed record for a steam train was set by a locomotive called the *Mallard*. It travelled at 126 miles an hour (203 kilometers an hour) while hauling seven coaches.

Many steam locomotives are now kept in museums. Try to visit a railroad or transportation museum to see them. You may even be able to travel on a working steam locomotive.

Find a model steam engine. Fill the boiler with water. Heat the boiler. **Take care,** especially if you are using methyl alcohol. How long does it take the boiler to build up steam? Watch how the connecting rod turns the wheel.

Electric power

Steam power was very useful in countries with plenty of coal. But some countries had no coal of their own. They had to buy their coal from other places. It became cheaper for these countries to use electricity to power their railroads. Today, electric power is used on many railroad routes.

One method of supplying electricity to a locomotive is to use overhead wires. These wires are supplied with electricity from power stations. The locomotives collect this electricity from the wires using a frame, called a pantograph.

Another method is to supply the electricity to a third rail. This is the conductor rail. A fourth rail can also be used. The locomotive is fitted with metal "shoes" to collect the power. How does your model train collect power?

Overhead wires

Pantograph

Third rail

When you are visiting railroad stations, look for these methods of using electric power. **Never** go near electric railroad lines.

Electric-powered locomotives are fitted with electric motors. The power, collected from overhead wires or the third rail, drives these motors. The motors drive wheels on the locomotives and enable them to move along the rails.

Find a small electric motor. Take the two wire leads and remove the plastic covering from the ends.

Make a switch, using a paper clip, two thumb tacks and a small block of wood. Connect one lead from the motor to the switch. Connect a length of wire from the other side of the switch to a 4.5 volt battery. Connect a lead from the motor to the battery.

Cut out a small cardboard "wheel." Find the center of the wheel and make a small hole. Push the spindle of the motor through this hole. Is it a tight fit? Switch on. Does the electric motor make the wheel turn?

Thumb tack — Paper clip

Paper clip switch

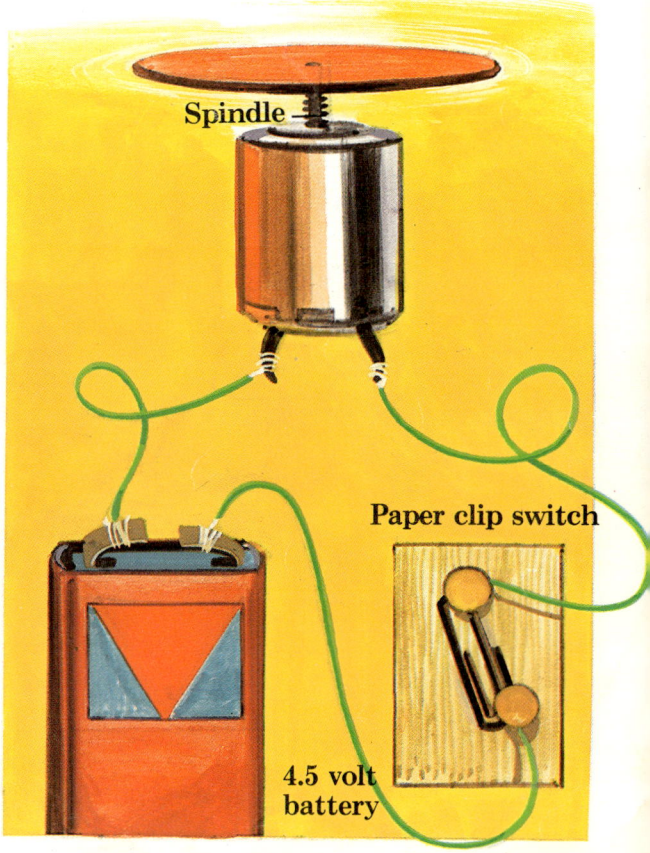

Spindle

Paper clip switch

4.5 volt battery

Diesel power

Many locomotives are driven by diesel engines. These powerful engines run on a fuel called diesel oil. Often the diesel engine in a locomotive operates an electric generator. This generator makes the electricity needed to drive electric motors. These motors drive the wheels. This type of locomotive is called a diesel-electric.

Look for diesel-electric locomotives in railroad stations. Are they pulling passenger cars? How many cars are in the longest train? Can you see diesel-electric locomotives pulling freight cars? Can you see diesel-electric locomotives doing any other jobs?

Chapter 5

Special trains

High-speed trains

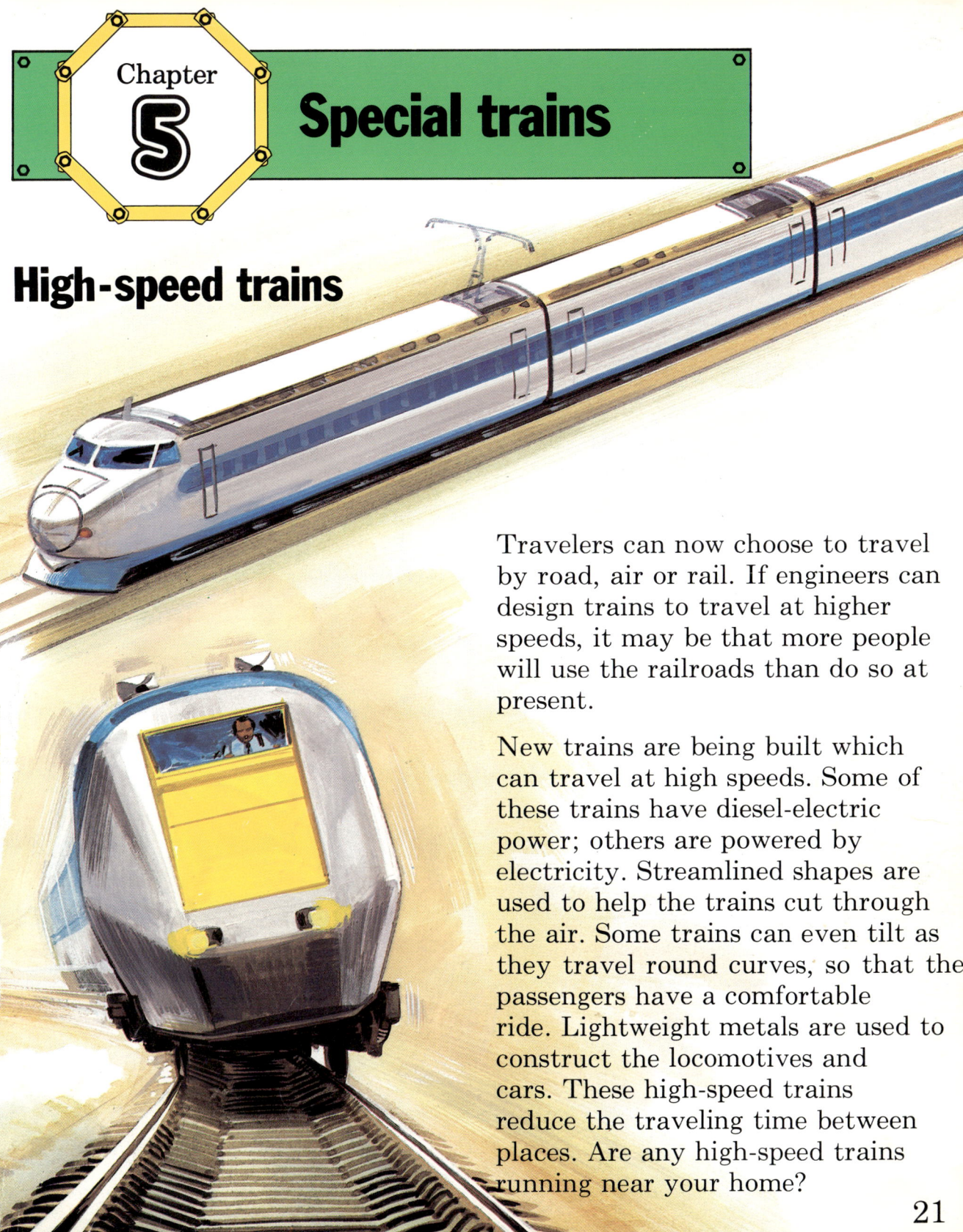

Travelers can now choose to travel by road, air or rail. If engineers can design trains to travel at higher speeds, it may be that more people will use the railroads than do so at present.

New trains are being built which can travel at high speeds. Some of these trains have diesel-electric power; others are powered by electricity. Streamlined shapes are used to help the trains cut through the air. Some trains can even tilt as they travel round curves, so that the passengers have a comfortable ride. Lightweight metals are used to construct the locomotives and cars. These high-speed trains reduce the traveling time between places. Are any high-speed trains running near your home?

Make a hovertrain

Another plan for a high-speed train uses the idea of an air-cushion. This wheelless train does not need railroad tracks. It runs on a concrete and steel spine. Motors make a cushion of air which lifts the train above the track. This reduces the amount of friction, which tends to slow up movement. (Friction normally occurs when train wheels run on steel rails.) Another motor pushes the train along at very high speeds. You can make a model hovertrain. Find a light polystyrene tray. Paint the tray so that it looks like a train. Make a small hole in the bottom of this tray. Cut a length of plastic tubing. Fit one end of the tubing into the hole in the tray. Blow through the tubing. This makes a cushion of air underneath the tray. Does your model lift off the floor?

Mag-lev trains

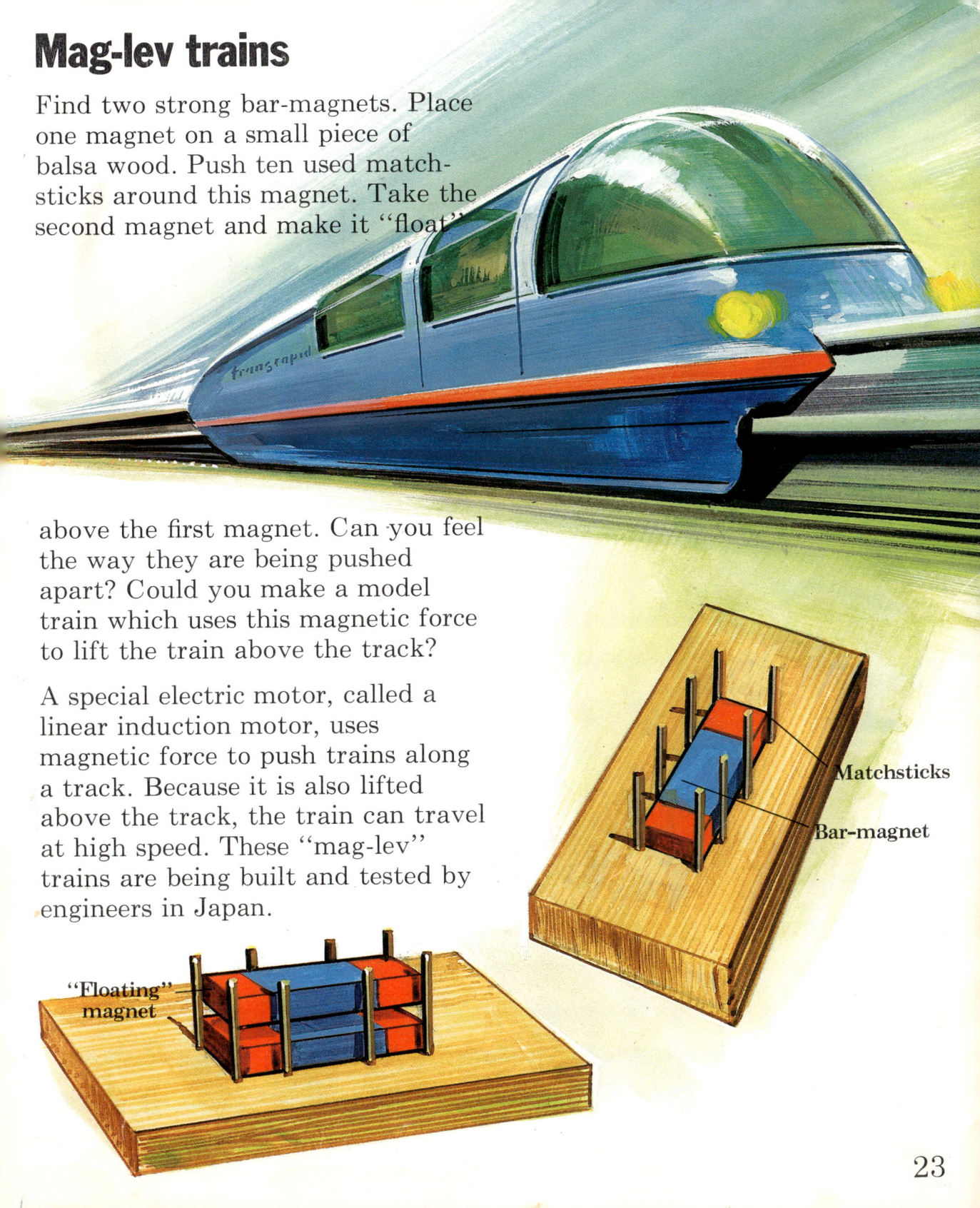

Find two strong bar-magnets. Place one magnet on a small piece of balsa wood. Push ten used matchsticks around this magnet. Take the second magnet and make it "float" above the first magnet. Can you feel the way they are being pushed apart? Could you make a model train which uses this magnetic force to lift the train above the track?

A special electric motor, called a linear induction motor, uses magnetic force to push trains along a track. Because it is also lifted above the track, the train can travel at high speed. These "mag-lev" trains are being built and tested by engineers in Japan.

Cable railways

Cable railways are used to provide transport up steep slopes, such as the side of a mountain. A passenger cable car is attached to a strong cable. An engine at the top of the mountain pulls the cable and cable car up the railway track. Often the cable cars work in pairs. One cable car travels up a track while another car travels down a parallel track. Sometimes water and gravity help to power cable railways.

Make a water-powered cable railway. Find two clean, plastic bottles. Paint each bottle to look like a passenger car.

Cut a small hatch in the base of each bottle. Now make two holes in the base of each bottle.

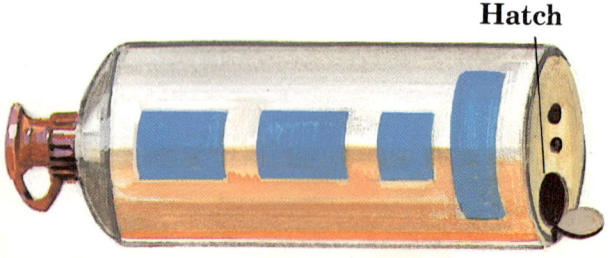
Hatch

Holes

Find a long plank of wood. Hammer two nails into one end of the wood. Fit empty thread spools over these nails. Make sure the spools can revolve easily.

Cut a length of string. Tie each end of the string through the holes in the bases of the plastic bottles. Position the model cable cars so that the string is around the two spools. Ask a friend to hold the wooden plank at an angle. Pull the string so that one cable car is near the top of the board.

Use a large jug to pour water through the hatch of the upper cable car. Does the upper car start to travel down the board? Why does this happen? Is the lower carriage being pulled up the board? When the first car reaches the bottom, let all the water escape. How can you pull this car back up the slope? Can you make rails and wheels for your model cable railway?

Monorail trains

Monorail trains travel on a single rail. Often this rail is built on supports above the ground. The trains either run on top of the rail or are suspended underneath it. They are powered by electric or diesel motors.

Monorail systems have been built in some cities. They provide a quick way of moving from place to place. Engineers do not need a lot of land to build the monorail track. This means that some monorails can be built along main streets. The buildings are left standing and cars, trucks and pedestrians can pass underneath.

Underground trains

The roads of most cities are crowded, so a fast train service is provided underground. Electric locomotives are usually used although the early subway trains were steam powered. What problems do you think this caused in tunnels?

To construct subway systems, engineers have to dig many tunnels. These may be just below the surface or at deeper levels. A new tunnel may have to be dug above or below an existing tunnel.

New subway stations have to be built. Escalators and elevators must be fitted so that people can travel between the different levels.

Have you traveled on the subway? How did you reach the subway platform? Did you think the trains were traveling fast?

Chapter 6: Safety on the railroads

Railroads and cold weather

Railroad engineers are always looking for ways of making trains safer and more reliable. Snow and ice cause great problems on the railroad. Engineers try to solve these problems and keep the trains running.

On electric railroads, ice on the third rail can stop the train from working. De-icing trains have to go along the track and spread special fluid on to the rail to keep ice from sticking to it.

In very cold weather, points can ice up and stop working. How have railroad engineers overcome this problem?

When it snows heavily, snowploughs are sent out to clear the lines. Make a snowplough for your model train out of one large piece of cardboard and two strips of cardboard. Attach them to the front of your locomotive with sticky tape. Scatter some small pieces of paper or polystyrene over your track. Does your snowplough clear away the "snow"?

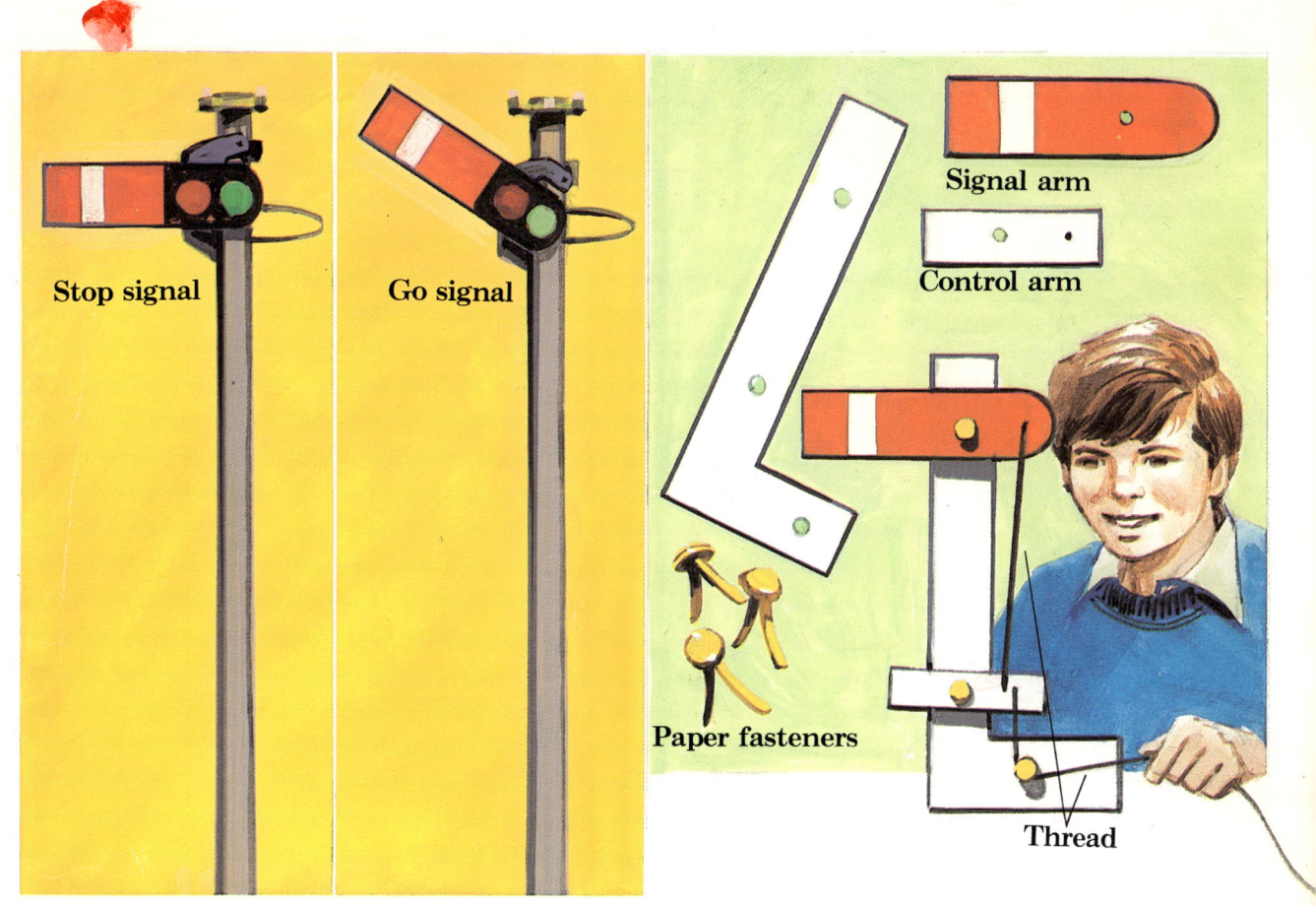

Simple signals

When you are traveling by train, look for signals along the side of the track. These signals tell the driver either to proceed or to stop.

Make a simple signal. Find a piece of thick cardboard and three paper fasteners. Cut out an L-shaped piece from the cardboard. Cut out two small strips of cardboard. Use one as a signal arm. Fasten it in position using a paper fastener. Use the other strip as the control arm. Fix this in place with another paper fastener. Push the third paper fastener into place below the control arm. Connect a piece of strong thread from the signal arm to the control arm. Attach another length of thread to the control arm. Run this thread around the third paper fastener.

Pull the end of this thread. What happens to the signal arm? Let go of the thread. What happens?

Make an electric signal

Electric light signals are used on many railroad systems. Often these are fixed to gantries above the railroad tracks.

Make an electric signal. Cut three pieces of wood to make a gantry. Use some nails and a hammer to fasten these pieces together.

Make a two-way switch, using three thumb tacks, a paper clip and a small piece of wood.

Wooden gantry

Two-way switch

Fasten two bulb holders on to the horizontal part of your wooden gantry. Connect one terminal of a 4.5 volt battery, with wire, to the thumb tack holding the paperclip switch. Connect the other battery terminal to each bulb holder. Connect each bulb holder to one of the thumb tacks of the switch. Screw a bulb into each bulb holder. Paint one bulb red and paint the other bulb green.

Use sticky tape to bind the wires to the wooden gantry. Test your circuit. The green light tells the driver it is safe to proceed. The red light tells the driver to stop. Use your electric signal gantry with a model railroad.

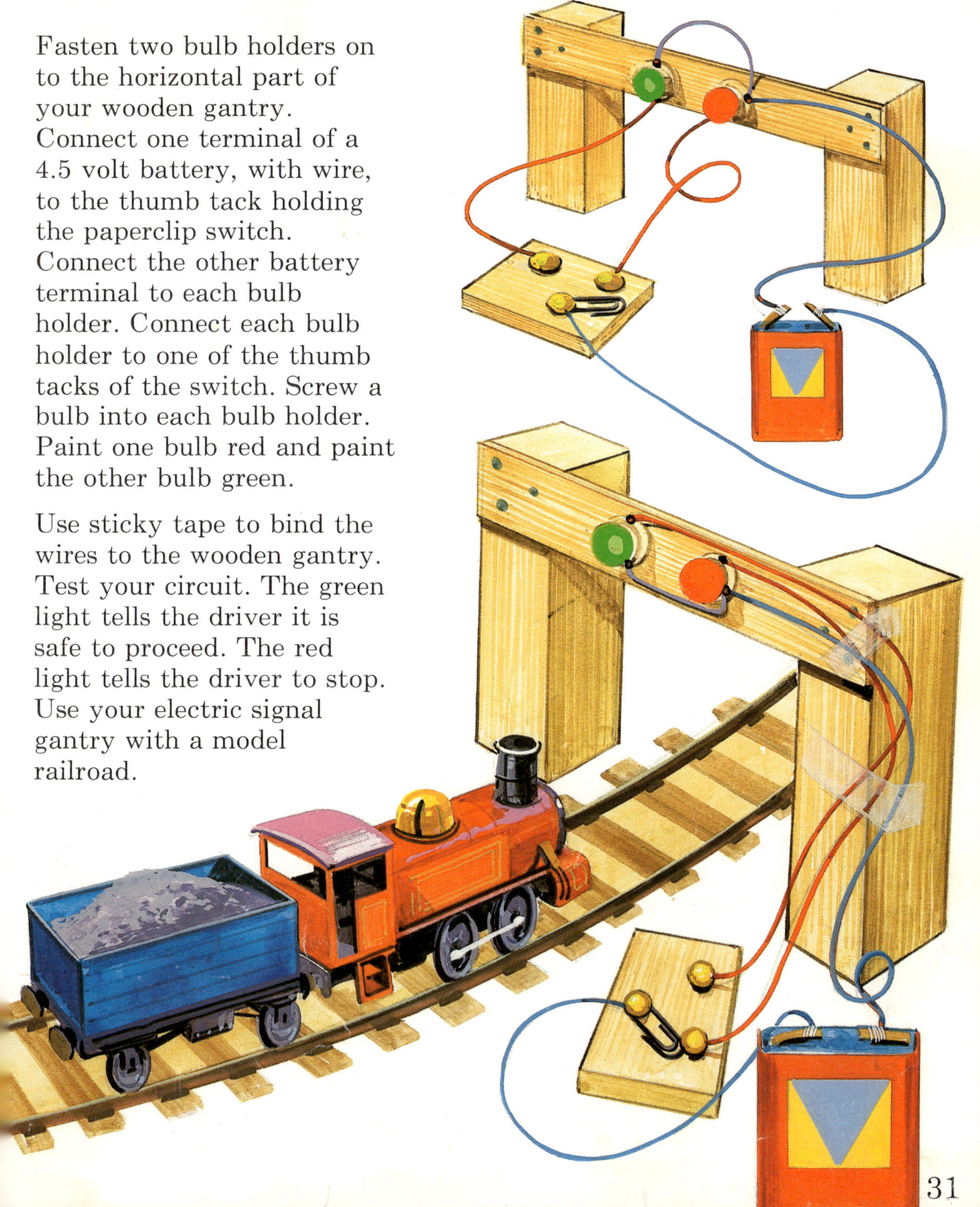

Automatic control

There have been terrible railroad accidents. Many of these have been caused by human errors. Engineers try to prevent accidents by using automatic safety devices on the track and in the locomotives. In one type of safety system, a horn sounds in the locomotive when the train passes a signal. If signals are ignored by the driver, then the train's brakes are automatically applied. This is very important when trains are traveling at higher speeds than ever before. Computers are now used to help engineers control trains.

They can control whole sections of track, even adjusting the speed of trains. Have you used a computer at home or in school?